My Daddy Loves Me

Written by
Kevin C. Grimes, Jr. &
Kevin C. Grimes, Sr.

Illustrated by Travis A. Thompson

ISBN: 979-8-218-39397-7

Published by:
Son of Tigga Publishing
www.sonoftiggapublishing.com

For:
(Kevin C. Grimes Jr.)
Mom and Dad, My Abuela Marcia and Grandpa Erick, TiTi Lorre, Titi Irene, Auntie Keisha, God Mothers Virgo & Bernice. My Godfather's DJ Supreme, Brian and Mark. My cousins Honesty, Madisyn and Peyton. And my Best Friend's Sky & Liam & Devin. To all my friends and family and teachers that support us.

(Kevin C. Grimes Sr.)
Mom and Dad, Tealie, Jakory & Joshua and My God Daughters Chelsea and Kaylah and Brianna and my God son Bradley & Brandon. To all my family and friends that support us. Salute to Brothers for life Brian, Rashion, Nigel , Mark , Ennis, Yoshi, Gary, Al

To my angels in heaven;
Shaki Young, Rodney Hearn, Garry Kirkland, Kelly Williams, Elizabeth Johnson, Ms Crystal Gumbs, Aunt Bell & Aunt Tee, Chuck Ross, Oneil Bandoo

Special thanks to Steven A. King

As the sun wakes me up.
I open my eyes in my cozy
room.
I stretch my arms way up
high as Dad stands in the
door way.

"Good morning, KJ. Time
to get up, son!"

"I know, dad, time to get
ready for school."

4

In the bathroom, I stand tall on my stool, singing the ABC song happily as I brush my teeth with my favorite blue toothbrush.

"A, b, c, d, e, f, g, h, i j, k, l, m, n,o..."

"Don't forget to brush your tongue," says KJ's dad.

"Yes, Dad, I already did...p, q, r, s, t, u, v, w, x, y, z."

ABC

Now I'm all dressed and ready for the day. I carefully walk down the stairs.

"Dad, I hope you made my favorite breakfast!"

"Pancakes, my favorite! You're the best dad!"

"Are you excited about school today?"

With a mouthful, "Yes, I have a test and we're going outside to play for recess."

"You are smart son, and I know you will do great on the test. Daddy has faith in you and loves you."

As me and my dad head to school in our shiny red truck, he asks me some math questions.

"Son, what is 10x10?"

"Dad, that's easy. It's 100"

"Okay, then what's 25x10?"

"Umm, umm ,umm, 250."

"Great job KJ. I like how you figured out the answer on your own without any help."

13

As we arrive at my school, my dad tells me to have a great day and listen to my teachers. We do our secret handshake and then I head off to school.

My dad yells, "KJ, guess what?"

"I know, I know. My daddy loves me!"

14

After a long day of learning and my dad's long day of selling houses, we are having my favorite for dinner tonight, pizza! We both are enjoying every bite, as I work hard on my homework.

"Dad do I add a period at the end of this sentence?"

"Yes, son and be careful the pizza is hot."

While I'm having the time of my life in my bubbly bath tub, here comes my dad!

"Five more minutes and it's time for bed."

19

Now I'm excited for my bedtime story. My dad is always filled with so much excitement while reading to me. He even makes funny voices that makes me laugh and giggle.

As I am falling asleep, I can hear him say, "Have a good night, son."

"Good night, Dad, and I know my daddy loves me!"

My Daddy Loves Me
Written By
Kevin C. Grimes, Jr. &
Kevin C. Grimes, Sr.
21

The End.